Baseball's
GREATEST
STARS

Andrew
McCUTCHEN

by Matt Scheff

SportsZone

An Imprint of Abdo Publishing
abdopublishing.com

abdopublishing.com

Published by Abdo Publishing, a division of ABDO, PO Box 398166, Minneapolis, Minnesota 55439. Copyright © 2016 by Abdo Consulting Group, Inc. International copyrights reserved in all countries. No part of this book may be reproduced in any form without written permission from the publisher. SportsZone™ is a trademark and logo of Abdo Publishing.

Printed in the United States of America, North Mankato, Minnesota
082015
012016

Cover Photos: John Bazemore/AP Images, foreground; Jeff Roberson/AP Images, background
Interior Photos: John Bazemore/AP Images, 1 (foreground); Jeff Roberson/AP Images, 1 (background); David Zalubowski/AP Images, 4-5; John Heller/AP Images, 6, 7; Seth Poppel/Yearbook Library, 8-9, 10-11; Tom Priddy/Four Seam Images/AP Images, 12-13, 14-15; Al Behrman/AP Images, 16-17; Gene J. Puskar/AP Images, 18-19, 24-25, 28-29; Dave Einsel/AP Images, 20-21; Tom Puskar/AP Images, 22; Helga Esteb/AP Images, 23; Jim Mone/AP Images, 26-27

Editor: Patrick Donnelly
Series Designer: Laura Polzin

Library of Congress Control Number: 2015945987

Cataloging-in-Publication Data
Scheff, Matt.
 Andrew McCutchen / Matt Scheff.
   p. cm. -- (Baseball's greatest stars)
Includes index.
ISBN 978-1-68078-077-2
1. McCutchen, Andrew (Andrew Stefan), 1986- --Juvenile literature. 2. Baseball players--United States--Biography--Juvenile literature.   I. Title.
796.357092--dc23
[B]   2015945987

CONTENTS

MAKING A SPLASH **4**

EARLY LIFE **8**

MINOR LEAGUE SENSATION **14**

BIG LEAGUER **18**

MOST VALUABLE PIRATE **22**

Timeline 30
Glossary 31
Index 32
About the Author 32

MAKING A SPLASH

Pittsburgh Pirates fans were buzzing on June 4, 2009. Their team was going for a sweep of the rival New York Mets. But the real draw was outfielder Andrew McCutchen. The team's top prospect was making his major league debut.

McCutchen did not let the fans down. He ripped a single to center field in his first at-bat. He came around to score later in the inning. And that was just the start.

It did not take long for McCutchen to hit his stride as a rookie.

McCutchen drew a walk in the fourth inning and scored another run. He singled again in the seventh. Then the speedy rookie thrilled the crowd by stealing second base. McCutchen came around to score on teammate Nyjer Morgan's triple. It was his third run of the day. The Pirates won the game 11-6 to sweep the Mets. The future looked bright for Pittsburgh's young superstar.

Morgan congratulates McCutchen after the rookie scored his first major league run.

McCutchen's teammates welcomed him to the Pirates with a shaving cream pie to the face after his first game.

FAST FACT
Four days after his debut, McCutchen had his first four-hit game. He had a single, a double, and two triples against the Atlanta Braves.

EARLY LIFE

Andrew Stefan McCutchen was born on October 10, 1986, in Fort Meade, Florida. His parents were still in high school. Both were excellent athletes. His mother, Petrina, played volleyball. His father, Lorenzo, was a football star. Lorenzo had dreams of playing in the National Football League. But Petrina persuaded him to become a minister instead. The couple married when Andrew was five.

FAST FACT

Andrew has one sibling—a younger sister named Lauren.

Andrew's parents were both star athletes when they were younger.

Andrew was a good student and star athlete. He made Fort Meade's high school varsity baseball team as an eighth grader. Andrew batted an amazing .591 that year. And he played more than just baseball. In track, he was part of a relay team that won the state championship. In football, he was a dangerous wide receiver and kick returner.

Andrew put up some incredible numbers during his high school days in Fort Meade, Florida.

11

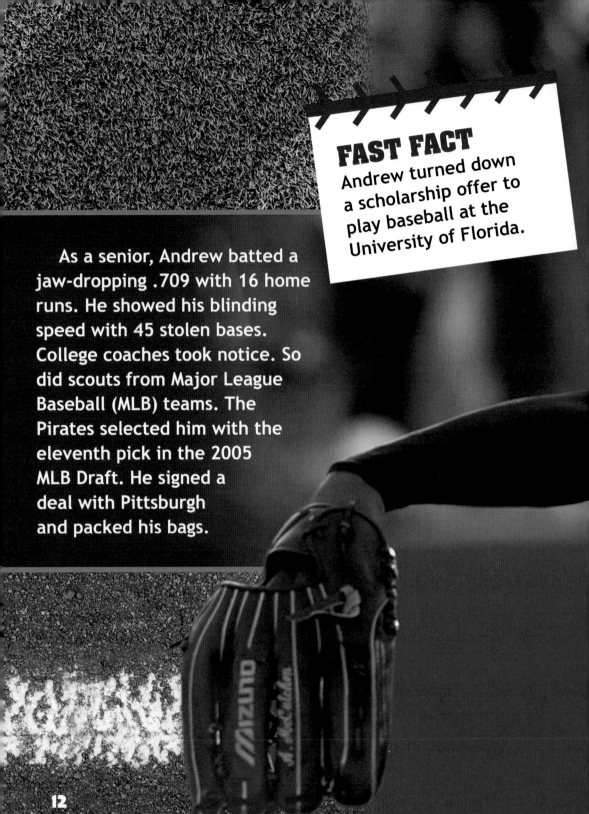

FAST FACT

Andrew turned down a scholarship offer to play baseball at the University of Florida.

As a senior, Andrew batted a jaw-dropping .709 with 16 home runs. He showed his blinding speed with 45 stolen bases. College coaches took notice. So did scouts from Major League Baseball (MLB) teams. The Pirates selected him with the eleventh pick in the 2005 MLB Draft. He signed a deal with Pittsburgh and packed his bags.

McCutchen warms up before a minor league game in 2006.

MINOR LEAGUE SENSATION

McCutchen reported to the Gulf Coast League Pirates to start his pro career in 2005 at age 18. He quickly rose through the Pirates' farm system. He batted .310 in 58 games that season. His first full season as a pro was 2006. McCutchen made the South Atlantic League's All-Star team. He also was named the Pirates' Minor League Player of the Year.

McCutchen's strong hitting and excellent speed helped him stand out in the minor leagues.

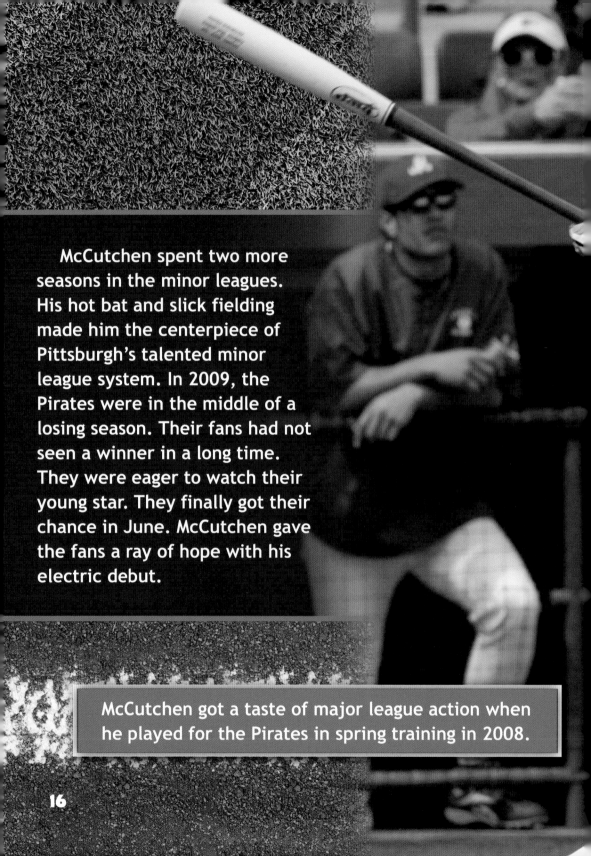

McCutchen spent two more seasons in the minor leagues. His hot bat and slick fielding made him the centerpiece of Pittsburgh's talented minor league system. In 2009, the Pirates were in the middle of a losing season. Their fans had not seen a winner in a long time. They were eager to watch their young star. They finally got their chance in June. McCutchen gave the fans a ray of hope with his electric debut.

McCutchen got a taste of major league action when he played for the Pirates in spring training in 2008.

BIG LEAGUER

McCutchen proved that he had been worth the wait. In 108 games as a rookie he batted .286 and slugged 12 home runs. In August he belted three home runs in a game against the Washington Nationals. A few weeks later, he launched a walk-off home run to lift the Pirates over the Philadelphia Phillies.

McCutchen blasts one of his three home runs against the Washington Nationals on August 1, 2009.

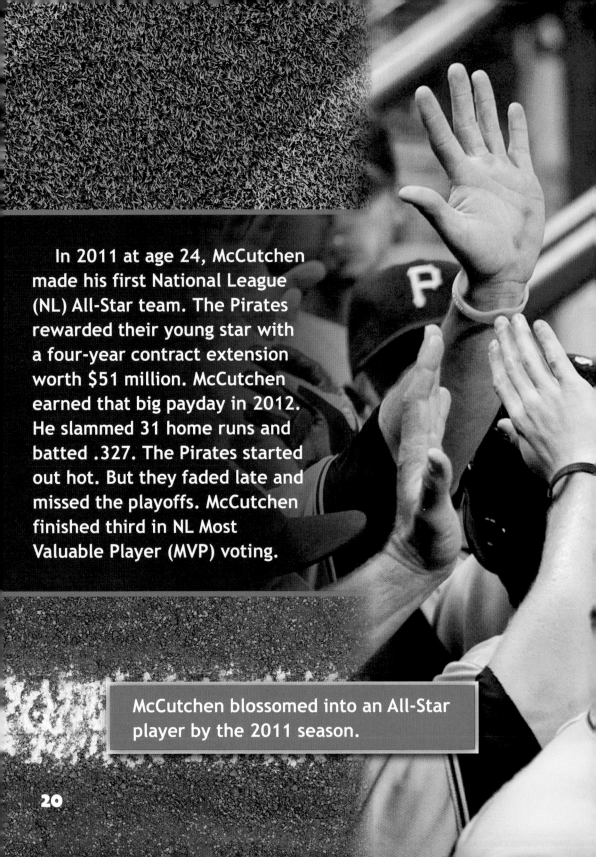

In 2011 at age 24, McCutchen made his first National League (NL) All-Star team. The Pirates rewarded their young star with a four-year contract extension worth $51 million. McCutchen earned that big payday in 2012. He slammed 31 home runs and batted .327. The Pirates started out hot. But they faded late and missed the playoffs. McCutchen finished third in NL Most Valuable Player (MVP) voting.

McCutchen blossomed into an All-Star player by the 2011 season.

21

MOST VALUABLE PIRATE

In 2013, Pittsburgh fans were hungry for a winner. The Pirates had not reached the playoffs since 1992. That was the second-longest streak in MLB. Fans thought McCutchen and his teammates could break the streak that season. And they did. With his outstanding fielding and timely hitting, McCutchen led the Pirates to the playoffs. He was rewarded with the NL MVP Award.

McCutchen and his teammates celebrate after beating the Cardinals in Game 3 of their NL Division Series.

McCutchen and Maria arrive at the 2013 American Music Awards.

FAST FACT

In December 2013, McCutchen proposed to his girlfriend, Maria Hanslovan, on *The Ellen DeGeneres Show*.

The Pirates faced the Cincinnati Reds in a one-game playoff. Pirates fans packed PNC Park in downtown Pittsburgh. McCutchen gave them plenty to cheer about. He reached base four times, with two hits and two walks. The Pirates won the game 6-2. "We're for real," McCutchen told reporters after the game. "We're definitely for real."

FAST FACT

The Pirates lost the 2013 NL Division Series to the St. Louis Cardinals, three games to two.

McCutchen hangs on the fence after a Cardinals home run in the 2013 NL Division Series.

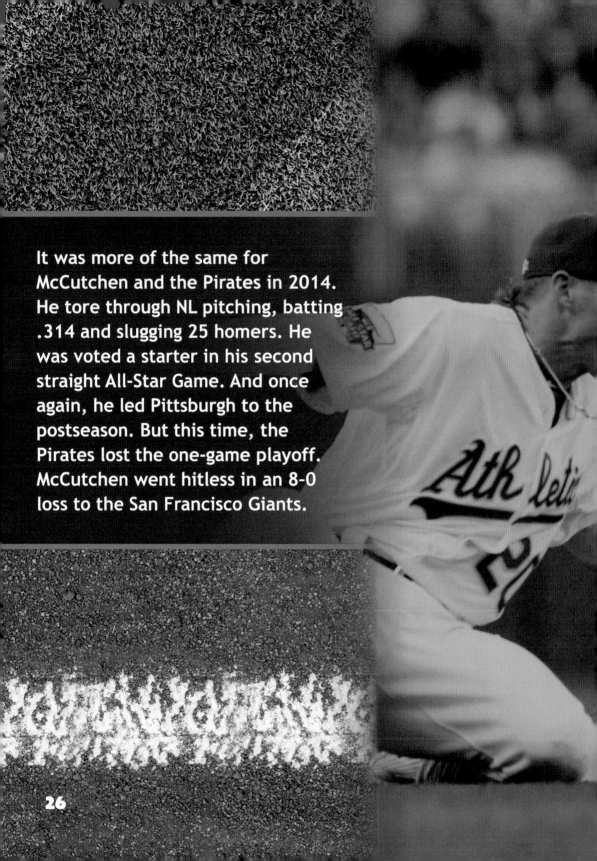

It was more of the same for McCutchen and the Pirates in 2014. He tore through NL pitching, batting .314 and slugging 25 homers. He was voted a starter in his second straight All-Star Game. And once again, he led Pittsburgh to the postseason. But this time, the Pirates lost the one-game playoff. McCutchen went hitless in an 8-0 loss to the San Francisco Giants.

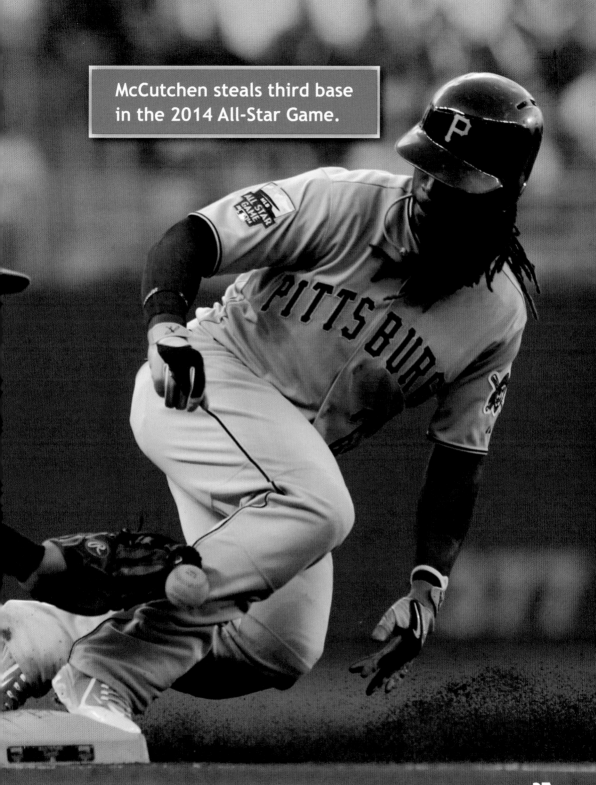

McCutchen steals third base in the 2014 All-Star Game.

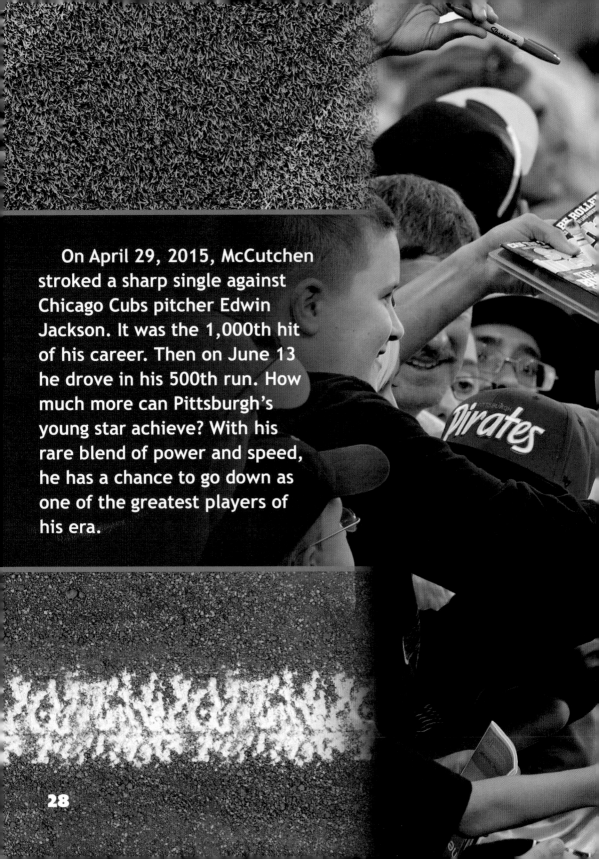

On April 29, 2015, McCutchen stroked a sharp single against Chicago Cubs pitcher Edwin Jackson. It was the 1,000th hit of his career. Then on June 13 he drove in his 500th run. How much more can Pittsburgh's young star achieve? With his rare blend of power and speed, he has a chance to go down as one of the greatest players of his era.

McCutchen is a fan favorite wherever he and the Pirates play.

TIMELINE

1986
Andrew Stefan McCutchen is born on October 10 in Fort Meade, Florida.

2005
The Pirates select McCutchen with the eleventh overall pick in the MLB Draft.

2006
McCutchen is named the Pirates' Minor League Player of the Year.

2009
McCutchen makes his major league debut with the Pirates.

2011
McCutchen makes his first NL All-Star team.

2012
McCutchen belts a career-high 31 home runs.

2013
McCutchen wins the NL MVP Award and leads the Pirates to a Wild Card playoff victory.

2014
The Pirates make the playoffs for the second straight season but lose to the Giants.

2015
McCutchen collects his 1,000th career hit and drives in his 500th career run.

GLOSSARY

CONTRACT
An agreement to play for a certain team.

DEBUT
First appearance.

DRAFT
The process by which leagues determine which teams will sign new players coming into the league.

FARM SYSTEM
In baseball, all the minor league teams that feed players to one major league team.

PROSPECT
An athlete likely to succeed at the next level.

ROOKIE
A first-year player.

SCHOLARSHIP
Money given to a student to pay for education expenses.

SCOUT
A person who evaluates talent and reports back to his or her employer.

SWEEP
Winning every game in a series.

WALK-OFF HOME RUN
A home run that puts the home team ahead in the final inning, forcing the players to walk off the field.

INDEX

Atlanta Braves, 7
awards, 14, 20, 22

Chicago Cubs, 28
Cincinnati Reds, 24
contract, 20

Fort Meade, Florida, 8

Gulf Coast League Pirates, 14

Hanslovan, Maria, 23

Jackson, Edwin, 28

McCutchen, Lauren, 8
McCutchen, Lorenzo, 8
McCutchen, Petrina, 8
Morgan, Nyjer, 6

National Football League, 8
New York Mets, 4, 6
NL All-Star team, 20, 26

Philadelphia Phillies, 18
playoffs, 20, 22, 24, 26
PNC Park, 24

San Francisco Giants, 26
South Atlantic League, 14
St. Louis Cardinals, 24

University of Florida, 12

Washington Nationals, 18

ABOUT THE AUTHOR

Matt Scheff is an artist and author living in Alaska. He enjoys mountain climbing, deep-sea fishing, and curling up with his two Siberian huskies to watch baseball.